It was raining, but the sun was
  shining at the same time.
The children looked up and saw a
  rainbow across the sky.
'I wonder where the rainbow begins?' asked Wilf,
  'and where it ends?'

1

In a place far away, there was a lorry.
It was a very big lorry because on the
   back was a very big machine.
The machine made rainbows and was called
   The Rainbow Machine.

There are seven colours in the rainbow.
It took seven people to look after the
 rainbow machine.
They cleaned it and polished it and
 they made sure it worked properly.

The rainbow machine had to be
   ready at any time.
Sometimes weeks and weeks went by and
   a rainbow was not needed.
But when the call came, the
   rainbow makers had to work fast.

Off they went in the lorry.
While it was going along, the rainbow
  makers got the machine ready.
Then, one .. two .. three .. Go!
They pressed a button and the rainbow
  shot out of the machine.

When there was a rainbow, everyone
  stopped to look at it.
Children ran to their mums or dads and said,
  'What a beautiful rainbow!'

Sometimes the rainbow was very bright but
  sometimes it was quite pale.
Often the children ran towards it.
They wanted to find the end of it, and
  play in all the colours.
But, of course, they never could.

One of the rainbow makers was a
   young man called Fred.
He was new and he was learning to be a
   rainbow maker.
One day, the other rainbow makers said,
   'Look after the lorry, Fred. We won't be long.'

8

The lorry was on a double yellow line.
Fred saw a traffic warden.
'Oh no!' said Fred. 'I must move
  the rainbow machine.'
So he climbed into the driver's cab and
  drove away.

Fred drove the lorry along the road.
'This is fun,' he said. 'But
I'd better not be too long.'
He wanted to turn the lorry round, so
he drove into a field.

Oh no! The lorry stuck in the mud.
The wheels spun round and round and
  the lorry sank deeper and deeper.
'Now what shall I do?' thought Fred.

Suddenly, there was a door in the field.
Biff and Chip came through it with
  Wilf, Nadim, and Anneena.
Biff had the magic key.
A new adventure had begun.

The children saw that a lorry was
  stuck in the field.
Then they saw Fred.
'Can you help me?' called Fred.
  'Will you push the lorry?'

The children pushed, but it was no good.
The lorry was too big, and it was
  far too heavy.
Suddenly, it began to rain even though the
  sun was shining.

On the lorry, things began to
  buzz and flash.
'Oh no! said Fred. 'A rainbow is needed.
This is The Rainbow Machine.
It makes rainbows.
You must all help me.'

The children helped Fred to pull the
cover off the rainbow machine.
'Wow!' said Biff. 'Is **that** where
rainbows come from?'
'Yes,' said Fred, 'but I don't know how to
work the computer yet.'

Nadim was good with computers.
He looked at the rainbow keyboard.
He didn't really know what to do, but
   he didn't like to tell Fred.
'Don't worry, I can work it,' he said.
'Right,' said Fred. 'One .. two .. three.'

The rainbow machine sent up a rainbow.
'Hooray! It's working,' said Wilf.
The rainbow was too bright for them to
  see it properly so Fred gave everyone
  some dark glasses.

The children looked up at the
   rainbow they had made.
It didn't look quite right.
Fred called to Nadim. 'Are you
   sure you can use that computer?'

The rainbow didn't look right.
First it went straight up.
Then it went straight along and
   then it went straight down.
'Oh dear,' gasped Anneena. 'It's
   got straight sides.'

Everyone stopped to look at the rainbow.
Children ran to their mums and dads.
'What a funny rainbow!' they said.
'It's got straight sides.
We've never seen one like that before.'

The rainbow makers were having a
  cup of tea.
They looked out of the window.
Everyone was staring at the sky.
'Oh no!' said the rainbow makers.
'What has Fred done?'

They ran out into the road but
  the rainbow machine had gone.
'Oh no!' said the rainbow makers.
'Where has Fred gone?'
In the sky was a broken rainbow.
'What a funny rainbow!' everyone said.

The rainbow changed again.
This time it was twisted and it
   was very bright.
'I like that one,' said a little boy.
'It looks wonderful.'

'We must find the rainbow machine,'
  called the rainbow makers.
They looked up at the sky.
The rainbow had changed again.
'Oh no!' said one of them.
'I don't want to look!'

Back at the rainbow machine, something
　had gone wrong.
Nadim had been too clever.
The rainbow was leaking and
　all the red was running out.

The sky was turning red.
'Oh no!' said Nadim. 'I can't stop the red.
Turn the rainbow machine off.'
Fred turned pale.
'I can't turn it off,' he said.

The rainbow makers found the lorry.
They were cross with Fred.
'It will take days to get the sky
　　blue again,' they said.

The rainbow machine had to
bleach the sky.
'We've never had to do this before,' said
one of the rainbow makers.
'I hope it works.'

The sky had turned white.
The sun wasn't yellow any more.
'It's a lot better than a red sky,'
  said one of the rainbow makers.
'A red sky makes everyone bad-tempered.'

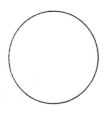

'We're very sorry,' said Nadim.
'It was all my fault.
Please don't blame Fred.'
'It's all right,' said the rainbow makers.
'The sky will soon turn blue again.'
Suddenly, the magic key began to glow.

The sky was blue and the sun was shining.
'The rainbow isn't really made like that, is it?'
  asked Kipper.
'You had better go to the end of one
  and find out,' said Anneena.